***** Five Stars (out of Five)
"These would be great plays at any moment. To be able to watch them now, brings some much-needed art into our days."
Whats On Stage (UK)

"Richard Nelson's haunting new play…. [A] sense of anxiety in the face of the unknown pervades this beautifully written…play."
Theater Pizzazz

"[A] masterful trilogy of plays created for Zoom… Both profound and engrossing."
Gay City News

"…The profound humanism that has informed the entire Apple cycle."
Lighting and Sound America

"Nelson's fantastic gift being the ability to summon the ways quotidian flotsam can merge with the Big Stuff."
Theater News Online

"Even more moving than its predecessors."
CurtainUp

"Like all of us, the Apples have been improvising through new experiences in 2020 and in that sense, there is a common humanity that bonds us all."
Broadway World

INCIDENTAL MOMENTS OF THE DAY premiered on The Apple Family Productions' YouTube Channel (Produced by Apple Family Productions, supported by Susie Sainsbury) on 10 September 2020. The cast and creative contributors were:

BARBARA APPLE	Maryann Plunkett
RICHARD APPLE	Jay O Sanders
JANE APPLE	Sally Murphy
TIM ANDREWS	Stephen Kunken
MARIAN APPLE	Laila Robins
LUCY MICHAEL	Charlotte Bydwell
Director	Richard Nelson
Production Stage Manager	Theresa Flanagan
Technical Director	Ido Levran
Choreography	Dan Wagoner
Dance Consultant	Gwyneth Jones
General Manager	Rebecca Sherman
Production Manager	Jeff Harris
Press Representative	Candi Adams
Company Manager	Anna Wheeler
Photographer	Jason Ardizzone-West

INCIDENTAL MOMENTS OF THE DAY

The Apple Family:
Conversations on Zoom

Part Three:
A Pandemic Trilogy

Richard Nelson

BROADWAY PLAY PUBLISHING INC
New York
www.broadwayplaypublishing.com
info@broadwayplaypublishing.com

Cover photo by Jason Ardizzone-West

First edition: December 2020
I S B N: 978-0-88145-891-6

Book design: Marie Donovan
Page make-up: Adobe InDesign
Typeface: Palatino

CHARACTERS

BARBARA APPLE, *high school English teacher, lives in Rhinebeck.*

RICHARD APPLE, *her brother, lawyer, retiring from the state's governor's office; lives in Albany, soon to move to Rhinebeck.*

MARIAN APPLE, *her sister, elementary school teacher.*

JANE APPLE, *her sister, a free-lance writer for local magazines.*

TIM ANDREWS, JANE'S *partner, manager of a Rhinebeck restaurant and part-time actor, lives in Rhinebeck, staying in his mother's house in Amherst, with his daughter, Karen, and her friend, Maggie.*

LUCY MICHAEL, *a former high school student of* BARBARA'S; *a dancer, and artistic director of her own dance company. Presently on a residency in France. Grew up in Rhinebeck.*

SETTING

Locations:

Five computer screens:

Rhinebeck, New York:

JANE *appears in the living room of her and* TIM's *apartment on South Street, Rhinebeck.*

MARIAN *appears in the living room of her house on Platt Street, Rhinebeck.*

Albany, New York:

BARBARA *and* RICHARD *appear in the living room of Richard's two-bedroom apartment in Albany.*

Amherst, Massachusetts:

TIM *appears in the bedroom he grew up in, in his mother's house in Amherst.*

Angers, France:

LUCY *appears in the dining area of the apartment where she has been staying since February, in Angers.*

Time: A day in early September 2020. 7:30PM-9PM

NOTE

I use a single quotation mark to notate when the character is paraphrasing, and double quotation marks when the character is actually reading from a source.

For Susie Sainsbury

1.
Yvonne.

(Two screens: BARBARA *and* JANE *in the middle of a conversation:)*

JANE: And Richard?

BARBARA: He seems happy.

(Then:)

JANE: And you?

BARBARA: What do you mean?

JANE: And you're all right?

BARBARA: Why do you ask me that?

JANE: You're there helping him pack. You're away from home. I know how you never like to sleep anywhere but your bed.

BARBARA: I've never said that. Never.

JANE: You have, Barbara, but—

BARBARA: *(Over this)* You make me sound like some—

JANE: You've said it.

BARBARA: —shut in. I go places. I have a life. A very interesting life. It may not be—I don't know— 'exotic'. My life hasn't been a series of— 'adventures'.

JANE: I'm sorry I asked…

BARBARA: *(Over this)* I'm fine. I'm good.

JANE: Great. I can't wait to meet Yvonne. She sounds like a lot of fun.

BARBARA: She is…

JANE: *(Again)* I can't wait to meet her.

(Short pause)

BARBARA: She's lived, lives an interesting life. And done so many things. You get intimidated.

JANE: Of course. I would. I will.

BARBARA: So you think that's normal too?

JANE: If she's done so many things, Barbara.

BARBARA: She tells great stories. They seem to just come right out of her. Pop right out. She told us one just now in Richard's car.

JANE: Coming back from your picnic?

BARBARA: Yeh.

(The story:)

Yvonne was in this play some years ago in New York. The play takes place in like 1958 in Greenwich Village. And—. Wait, before I tell you that.

JANE: Tell me what?

BARBARA: She told us two things, both interesting. Throughout the play there are sounds of the city—a city 'soundscape', she called it: street noise, car horns, firetrucks… After the show there's a talk with the audience and one person in the audience raises his hand and says, 'you know that firetruck noise, did you know that's from a—and names some kind of fire truck— 'which we did not have in the department until 1961'.

JANE: He'd been a fireman.

BARBARA: Yeh. She said, people are always bringing their own lives into a play. Their own experiences or assumptions…

JANE: Did they change the sound of the firetruck?

BARBARA: Probably not. Anyway, here's the story I started to tell. A young woman in the audience, in the talk after the show, raises her hand, and complains *(In a voice:)*
'I found the play unbelievable', the woman says. Yvonne did a funny voice.

JANE: She's an actress.

BARBARA: *(Over this)* The woman continues *(A voice)*, 'The girl in the play—she's fifteen—she goes to Poughkeepsie and buys herself a diaphragm. A fifteen-year-old girl in 1958 wouldn't be able to buy herself a diaphragm in a place like Poughkeepsie. I didn't believe it for a minute!'
(Then)
The rest of the audience, Yvonne says, starts nodding their heads, agreeing, some even applauding. *(In a voice)*"This play has a big flaw!" When another woman—.

JANE: What?

BARBARA: —in the audience, an older woman, raises her hand and she says, 'I know this is going to be hard to believe but, I grew up upstate, and when I was fifteen, which by the way was in 1958, I went to Poughkeepsie, and there I bought my first diaphragm.'

JANE: You're kidding?

BARBARA: No.

JANE: *(Over this)* What are the odds…?

BARBARA: Stories like that just pop out of her…

JANE: What role was Yvonne playing in the diaphragm play?

BARBARA: I don't know, Jane. Why does it matter? Now the movers are coming on Tuesday. Richard needed an extra day. He wants to be here for that.

JANE: I would too. But you have school…

BARBARA: I'll come back to Rhinebeck in the morning. He says if he needs help, he's got Yvonne…
(Stops and listens)
I thought that was Richard… No.
(New story)
Jane, this is the most incredible thing I've heard in my three days here.

JANE: What did she say?

BARBARA: Not her. No. Our brother. The lawyer. I heard him say out loud—out of his own mouth—this to Yvonne. He just tossed it out there…

JANE: What?

BARBARA: That maybe he'll try out for some show at the Rhinebeck Theater Society.

JANE: What? No. To do what?

BARBARA: To act in, Jane. Act, our brother! He said that over dinner last night at Yvonne's. Just casually…

JANE: He doesn't even like the theater.

BARBARA: *(Over this)* I almost choked. He asked her—

JANE: Yvonne.

BARBARA: *(Over this)* —to keep any eye out for a role that— 'might be good for him…'

JANE: *(Laughing)* I can't believe this…

BARBARA: I was there. He said it with a straight face. He wasn't joking.

JANE: Maybe—

BARBARA: *(Laughing)* What?

JANE: *(Laughing)* Maybe he could play—what did Benjamin play when he couldn't remember anything?

BARBARA: Ghost of Christmas Future! That part has no lines. Good idea.

JANE: *(Over this)* Yes that! He can play that!

BARBARA: *(Same time)* Let him play that...

(They calm down.)

JANE: He's going to be one of those amateur actors who thinks he's good, just because he's been a lawyer...

BARBARA: I know. I know.

(Then)

JANE: They're trying to do them outside now. The plays...

BARBARA: And how's that working out?

JANE: *(Shrugs)* So what's her house like?

BARBARA: Tasteful. She's got good taste, Jane. Great taste...

JANE: So, expensive?

BARBARA: Not necessarily. It's small. Good for 'weekends'. Summers. Oh and she's going to come down and help him with his new house...

JANE: Of course she is.

BARBARA: *(Over this)* No, I suggested it. Richard was surprised, he said 'I thought you wanted to help me with that, Barbara?'

(TIM appears on his screen:)

TIM: I'm here! What time is it? I fell asleep...

BARBARA: *(Over this)* Look who's here.

JANE: Why were you sleeping?

TIM: You aren't waiting for me?

BARBARA: Lucy text-ed, she won't be ready until about eight-thirty now.

TIM: Should I come back?

JANE: Tim.

TIM: What?

JANE: Why do you say that?

BARBARA: Of course you shouldn't come back. Now that you're here…
(*She stands.*)
I'm warming up last night's dinner.

TIM: What did you have, Barbara?

BARBARA: Richard and Yvonne cooked. It was great. A summer pasta dish. I asked for the recipe… What are you eating, Jane?

JANE: (*Defensive*) I made myself a salad…

BARBARA: And Tim?

TIM: I'm good.

JANE: I thought you ate at Yvonne's last night.
BARBARA: She sent us home with a doggy bag. You two talk. Tim—Jane. Jane—Tim…
(*She goes.*)

(*Then*)

JANE: Where are you? Where is that?

TIM: In my old bedroom.

JANE: Right…

TIM: I let the girls have the master bedroom.
(*A joke*)
I'm back where I started, Jane. Same damn room.

JANE: I know the room, Tim… I've been there.
(*Short pause*)
Say hi to Karen and Maggie…

(TIM *nods.*)

JANE: Not that they're so interested in hearing from me.

TIM: They're out walking around. I think they're pretending to be college students in a college town.

JANE: They're old enough.

TIM: (*To say something*) Amherst is crazy. And getting crazier. The students are almost all here but they don't go to class.

JANE: Why are they there?

TIM: I suppose the colleges want to make money…

JANE: So they're like resorts now?

TIM: It does feel like that.

(*Neither knows what to say, then:*)

JANE: Marian was here… She just left.

TIM: In our apartment?

JANE: And inside.

TIM: Wow. No masks?

JANE: (*Over this*) She came inside.
(*Obviously*)
We had masks. Just for a few minutes, mostly we stood outside. She was all dressed up. She needed to look in a mirror. She was going on a date.

TIM: The dog walker's back?

JANE: Another one, Tim. She wasn't sure where he was taking her. She thought maybe the Beekman. Under their tent on the lawn. She's talked a few times to the guy. They've taken walks. Meet at the Mills and walk—six feet apart. Masks… Tim?

TIM: What?

JANE: She said, she's really looking forward to having a meal with him. Because she'll finally get to see his face. She's never seen his face...

TIM: *(As he looks at his watch)* That's funny.

JANE: You have to go somewhere?

TIM: Not yet.

JANE: And why were you taking a nap?

TIM: You try living with these kids...

JANE: Yvonne told Barbara how she and Richard met. You want to know? You'll be interested. You're an actor...

TIM: How?

JANE: Richard was at party in Albany. This was long ago when you could go to people's houses. Remember that time?

TIM: Another world. Another time.

JANE: Richard's in the kitchen and this woman comes in.

Yvonne. She's looking for him. 'Are you Mr Apple?' 'Yes.' He says, 'I'm Richard.' And she says, Tim, 'Are you any relation to the actor, Benjamin Apple?'

TIM: To Benjamin?

JANE: She'd acted with Uncle Benjamin, Tim.

TIM: That's neat.

JANE: Two, three times. Isn't that amazing...

TIM: He knew a lot of actors, Jane.

BARBARA: *(Off)* What took you so long? *(Calls)* Richard's back!!

JANE: Richard's back.

TIM: I didn't know he'd gone anywhere.

JANE: *(Over this)* From taking his girlfriend home.

BARBARA: *(Off)* They're already on, Richard.

JANE: Tim, you never take naps. How late do they stay up?

(RICHARD appears, leans down and talks:)

RICHARD: Jane. Tim.

TIM: Richard.

BARBARA: *(Off)* Where were you?

RICHARD: *(To BARBARA)* I wasn't that long...

BARBARA: *(Off)* Marian's on a date. You missed her. I'm getting our dinner.

RICHARD: *(To BARBARA)* What about the dance?

BARBARA: *(Off)* It's not for a while now...

RICHARD: *(To BARBARA)* And I rushed back.

BARBARA: *(Off)* Lucy text-ed, she wasn't ready...I told you not to rush!

JANE: Tim, Marian asked if you could record the dance...

BARBARA: *(Off)* And for Yvonne.

RICHARD: *(As he sits)* Jane, so who's Marian's date?

TIM: Not the dog walker.

JANE: She won't give a name.

BARBARA: *(Appears)* She says he has cute eyebrows. That's all we know.
(She goes off again.)

JANE: You get Yvonne home all right?

RICHARD: She needed a rest...

BARBARA: *(Reappearing)* We invited her to watch the dance… But she was too tired.

(Lights fade.)

2.
Depressions.

(RICHARD and BARBARA eating, in Albany. TIM sits in his old bedroom in Amherst. JANE in her living room in Rhinebeck. The middle of a conversation:)

BARBARA: *(To RICHARD)* Don't eat so fast.

JANE: He didn't look like a redneck, Tim. He looked normal, like us. Nice shirt. A little older.

BARBARA: *(Eating)* This was in Tops?

JANE: This morning, Barbara.

TIM: You went shopping?

JANE: Yes. I do that, Tim. I have to eat.

RICHARD: And he wasn't wearing a mask.

JANE: No.

TIM: Good for you.

JANE: *(To TIM)* Why do you say it like that?

TIM: I just said— 'good for you…'

BARBARA: *(To RICHARD)* Inside you have to wear—.

RICHARD: Who enforces that, Barbara? No one enforces that.

BARBARA: Jane, did anyone say anything--?

JANE: To the mask-less man? No. Nothing. He just kept appearing every time I turned into another aisle. When I had to pass him I held my breath.

BARBARA: Last week at Tops, one of the guys working there, he was stocking the frozen foods, and I watch him give out this huge sneeze. Ca-choo!! Right into the freezer…I didn't buy anything frozen…

TIM: Jane, I'm just happy you're getting out.

JANE: Fuck…
(She stands.)
I'll get my salad…
(As she goes:)
And I see people. Marian was just over.
(She is gone.)

RICHARD: How are the girls, Tim?

TIM: I was just explaining to Jane, Amherst is a strange place right now. The students are here—.

BARBARA: Are they?

TIM: They're here. Most of them. But they take their classes online.

BARBARA: Then why are they there?

RICHARD: *(Eating, obviously)* Money…

TIM: In a funny way, it's like the girls are here going to college… And not taking the year off…. They're never home. I don't know where they go or what they do…
(JANE returns with her salad.)

RICHARD: Keep them away from your Mom. If they're going out like that.

BARBARA: Tim can't even see his Mom, Richard.

JANE: You wave through a window…

TIM: She sees me… We wave. Her home has yet to have single case.

JANE: Knock wood.

TIM: *(Same time)* Fingers crossed.

RICHARD: Then they shut down in time… Unlike in our state… Here we sent the infected right back in…

BARBARA: Richard…

RICHARD: Just making a point.

BARBARA: What point?

RICHARD: Sending people with the virus back into nursing homes, was a very ill-advised decision. That's all, Barbara.

TIM: Come on, Richard. Give Cuomo a break.

RICHARD: Oh I have, many many times, Tim.

BARBARA: *(Explaining to* TIM*)* The Governor has never responded to Richard's letter -- resigning. An assistant—

RICHARD: Secretary. A secretary, Barbara.

BARBARA: *(Over this)* An assistant sent Richard some form to fill out.

RICHARD: Cuomo's too busy.
(Gestures with his hand: busy talking)

BARBARA: Richard…

RICHARD: I'm sure he's happy to get rid of me.

BARBARA: You keep saying that.

RICHARD: If Andrew Cuomo is now 'Our voice of empathy…' God help us. I tell everyone who'll listen, be leery of a leopard changing his spots…

BARBARA: So he didn't write you a stupid letter. You've always said he has thin skin. You walked away. That's how he sees things. Forget him.

RICHARD: *(Over the end of this)* I should have just followed my instinct and made as much fucking money as I possibly could.

BARBARA: That's not you, Richard. And never was.

RICHARD: Yvonne can't believe all the shit I've taken from him.

BARBARA: It's over. And you did a lot of good things…

(Then)

JANE: *(New subject)* Barbara, you know I realized today, Marian and I were just talking about it, that when Richard moves to his new house, it will be the first time when all four of us have lived in the same town since we were kids…

BARBARA: He's been staying with me.

JANE: As a guest, Barbara…

BARBARA: *(Standing)* Wine, Richard?

RICHARD: Let me get it. There's a bottle open in the fridge…

BARBARA: I'm up. I'm up.

RICHARD: Barbara, maybe a beer…

(BARBARA starts to go.)

JANE: *(Over this)* Tim…I already told you this, Barbara…

(BARBARA stops to hear.)

JANE: Marian heard today that Patricia Gabriel died in her nursing home in Poughkeepsie…

RICHARD: Who's—?

TIM: A neighbor. She wasn't young.

BARBARA: *(Over this)* I don't think you knew her, Richard.

TIM: She went to that nursing home, remember, because it would take Medicaid…

JANE: Happened two months ago. Marian just heard today. Patricia's daughter-in-law told her.

The daughter-in-law, Marian said, is furious… Our dumbass leader…' she's calling him.

RICHARD: Cuomo or Trump?

JANE: Blaming him.

BARBARA: *(Over this, to* RICHARD*)* She meant Trump, for Christ sake.
(She goes off.)

RICHARD: I was joking.

(Then)

TIM: Does Marian still have her Bernie sign on her lawn?

RICHARD: It was there a few days ago… When we left.

TIM: There was that one Trump sign in the village…

JANE: It's still there….

TIM: Only one. That says something.

RICHARD: We're in New York. What does it say?

JANE: *(Eating)* Tim, I saw this lecture. A talk. The Rhinecliff Library streamed it. A local person, a history-buff, like Richard.

*(*BARBARA *is returning with her wine and a beer.)*

JANE: I got Barbara to watch it too.

BARBARA: What?
(She sits back down.)

JANE: The return of Layfette.

BARBARA: This was interesting.

JANE: I hadn't know anything about this.

RICHARD: I've read about this, Jane.

BARBARA: Richard, let Jane. *(To* JANE*)* Tell Tim…

JANE: Years and years after the Revolution, Lafayette comes back to America, now an old man. He'd been made a general when he was only nineteen?

TIM: I didn't know that.

JANE: Now an old man. So you know all about this, Richard?

RICHARD: I'd read about it, but tell us…

BARBARA: Tell us, Jane…

JANE: Lafayette's broke. He'd almost been guillotined in his own revolution in France. Lost all of his money. His wife has died. He was in prison for years. And some American friends come up with a scheme to help him out. The President at the time, I forget who it was—. Richard?

RICHARD: I don't remember either…

JANE: He invites Lafayette back to America—offers to send a ship to France just to pick him up. The speaker described America as going through a very difficult time then. There was the sense that we'd lost our way, somehow. And—this was a presidential election year too!

BARBARA: I think that's why she gave the talk.

JANE: You're right. She even said that. The presidential candidates of course each tried to tie themselves to Lafayette's return.

TIM: Why not?

RICHARD: Nothing changes, Tim.

JANE: So Lafayette arrives in New York and there are these dinners, and so forth. And then—there's a boat trip, on a steamboat, up the Hudson River. Right by us. He stopped for lunch at what's now the Mills Mansion, Richard.

RICHARD: That I didn't know.

JANE: As his ship heads north to Albany, crowds line the banks. Thousands. Tens of thousands of people. They come from everywhere. Wait for days. Someone's been by and sold fireworks, so there are fireworks. Songs in his honor have been written, and so crowds sing. Cannons are shot off. Boats form an armada.
(Then)
The speaker, she asked: Had a nerve been touched…? Or a need? What were all those people looking for? Something they'd lost? Forgotten? Or maybe they were just feeling leaderless?
(Short pause)
Tim, this boat trip, it all happened, in September. So there's an anniversary right around the corner… Next couple of weeks. I pitched this to the Chronogram and now they're letting me do an article.

TIM: That's fantastic, Jane. I didn't know—.

RICHARD: *(Over this, to* BARBARA*)* She's writing.

JANE: I'm finding photos online of stuff commemorating the event. Plates with Lafayette's face. Pitchers, bottles, coins, ribbons…

TIM: That's so great.

JANE: You think so?

TIM: I do… Good for you.
(They eat.)

JANE: And, Tim, I was just telling Marian when she was here, I'm thinking of taking an online training course to become a crisis counselor right now.

TIM: When did this—?

JANE: I read about it, Tim. It sounds like something I could do… And do well.

BARBARA: Tell Tim what it is. What you would do. *(To* RICHARD*)* I told you this.

JANE: People are having trouble—with all sorts of things right now.

BARBARA: They certainly are.

JANE: So you talk to them at any time of the day or night. They can call anytime. And you listen. It's the listening. That's the training. Until you can hook them up with a professional. People need to talk...

TIM: What's the training like?

JANE: I don't know yet. I just read about it. And it sounds interesting. You look surprised?

TIM: I'm not.

JANE: I know you think I'm depressed.

TIM: I've never said that word, Jane.

JANE: No, you haven't. And I am. I admit that.

BARBARA: She has said that word to me...

JANE: I read how the job of the crisis counselor is first and foremost, this was online: 'to persuade, with almost religious devotion' —they used that phrase— 'persuade the caller, the sufferer, of life's worth.' I want to do that. I want to be able to do that. I want to persuade someone of that.
(Then)
I also found online a chat you could take part in. For those curious and interested in the course. It's free...

TIM: You took part in this chat?

JANE: I will. And I realized I do some of these things that you're supposed to look out for. I have sometimes a crazy attachment to— *(Shrugs)* —silly things. My reading glasses. You've seen that, Tim.

TIM: I have...

JANE: If for a moment I don't know where they are…
This is pretty common. Attachments to silly things.
Small things. And so that's something you can say to a
caller—that what they're feeling -- it's pretty common.
(Then)
(Another)
That feeling of being followed. Not by someone.
That's paranoia. No, feeling you're being followed by
yourself. A second self—who watches you, observes
you with total calm and curiosity.
(She looks at her watch.)
What time is the dance?

BARBARA: Lucy won't be on for another half hour or
so… What else?

(Then)

JANE: Tim, I had my first dream this week, in months.
That I remember.
(Then)
Remember what Benjamin used to say? When he'd lost
his memory?

RICHARD: He said a lot of things, Jane.

JANE: He said, 'I forget how to remember.' That's what
it started to feel like. Days just slipping along and like
in a circle.
(She gets up.)

TIM: What are you doing?

JANE: I'm going for some wine… *(Joke)* Tim, you want
some?
(As she goes off:)
Oh, that's right, you're not here…
(She is gone.)

BARBARA: She's doing good, Tim.

TIM: I can see that.

RICHARD: And are you all right, Tim? How are you doing?

TIM: *(Shrugs)* I'm sitting in the same bedroom I had when I was five years old, Richard. There are photos of me in all my high school plays. Every now and then something catches my eye and I want to throw up...
(Smiles)
I'm okay...
(Shrugs)
They had an argument. My daughter and Jane...

BARBARA: I know. It happens.

TIM: She seems better.

RICHARD: Jane or your daughter?

TIM: Jane. But then again, I don't really know...

BARBARA: I make sure to see her every day... And while I'm here, Marian's checking in on her...

(JANE is returning with her wine:)

JANE: Before you dragged Barbara to Albany, Richard...

RICHARD: I didn't drag her—.

JANE: The two of us took a walk through your cemetery.

BARBARA: It's not his—.

JANE: We had masks, kept our distance—

BARBARA: I know what you're going to say...

JANE: No one's around. So you can speak loudly. And Barbara said, 'you know what I miss right now? More than anything? I miss people having a sense of humor... Have we all just lost our sense of humor?'

RICHARD: Cuomo thinks he's a funnyman.

BARBARA: Richard.

JANE: So Barbara and I came up with this… And we got Marian involved—that every day, we'd send each other a joke. Or some funny story…

RICHARD: I didn't know about this. Why didn't you ask me?

BARBARA: You'd just judge the jokes, Richard… And that sort of kills the point.

RICHARD: When do I do that?

JANE: So I'm thinking that this is something I'll suggest when I take this counseling course. That we also tell jokes or sweet stories to the people who call. If we feel it's right. At least to have them handy… Ready…

(Then)

BARBARA: Yvonne told me a joke just last night.

RICHARD: When did she—?

BARBARA: When you were in the kitchen making your fancy dressing. She just comes right out with things. *(Then)*
A young man is walking down the street—.

RICHARD: You're going to tell her joke?

BARBARA: Am I allowed to do that?

RICHARD: Sure, but—

BARBARA: I know I won't tell it as well as Yvonne, Richard.

RICHARD: I didn't say anything, Barbara.

BARBARA: If you don't want me to tell it.

RICHARD: Tell the joke.

BARBARA: Okay. I will. I am. Yvonne's joke. *(Then)*
So the young man is walking down a street in a city. Or a town. Past an apartment building. And suddenly

he hears a woman calling or yelling from above, 'Help. Help'. The man looks up and there's this woman on a balcony and she's the one shouting…
(Then)
And she's shouting—. Wait, first, you need to know that she has a glass eye. And so she's shouting, 'help, help, my glass eye has fallen out!'
(She looks at RICHARD.*)*

RICHARD: I'm listening.

BARBARA: *(Continues)* And the young man sees the eye falling and catches it; Yvonne said he dove and caught it. And that it was an amazing catch. Anyway, so he saves the glass eye… And he goes into the apartment, climbs the stairs and meets the woman and gives her back her glass eye. And she's very thankful. And also—and I should have said this already—she's very beautiful.
(Then)
So the young man sort of falls for her and asks her out on a date. And they go out to dinner, somewhere, I think Yvonne said 'candlelight'. That kind of dinner. And they end up in bed. And they make love. And the man is totally smitten with her. And so lying there in bed, it's now morning. Yvonne said the light was streaming through curtains… She made it sound very romantic. So—they're lying in bed and he asks her, 'so have you had many affairs before me?'
(Then)
And she says…
(She starts to laugh before saying the punch line.)
It's silly but it's funny.

RICHARD: Just tell us, Barbara.

BARBARA: I want to say it right. So 'have you had many affairs? And she says, 'only with those who catch my eye.'

(Laughs, then corrects herself)
'Caught my eye.' 'Caught my eye.' Yvonne said,
'caught my eye.' Either works…
(Then)
(To RICHARD*)*
I think Yvonne told it better…

(Lights fade.)

3.
What Are We Left With?

(BARBARA, RICHARD, TIM *and* JANE *in the middle of
conversation…)*

BARBARA: She said, "Barbara, I don't think just being
white makes me a racist. What do you think?"

RICHARD: And what did you say to Margaret?

BARBARA: I nodded. I agreed. She wanted to talk. I let
her talk.
(Then)
'I want to stand up for myself,' she said. 'Defend
myself. Stand up for what I really think and know
about myself. But I think if I did, I'd risk…'

RICHARD: Being lumped with… Yeh.

BARBARA: 'With people I hate,' she said.

RICHARD: Right.

TIM: I see that.

BARBARA: 'So what do I do, Barbara? What do we do?
Just shut up?'

JANE: Does she know about your problems with your
former students?

BARBARA: She does, Jane.
(Then)

Richard, I don't think Margaret was thinking about
making speeches or anything like that.
(To all of them:)
She meant, I'm sure, just talking about all this with
family or friends quietly, privately, in say a friend's
backyard. We were in my backyard.
(Then)
I asked her how much news she watches.

RICHARD: Good question.

BARBARA: She watches a lot. Too much. Like all of us.
And so yes she knows that there are very good reasons
for people being angry, and feeling hurt. Important
reasons, deep, profound, necessary, 'historical' reasons.
And for people wanting to right these obvious wrongs.
She knows that, she has those feelings, and wants that
too.
(Then)
But now, some of what is being done in the name of
that, being demanded in the name of all of that, she
really disagrees with. But how do you say that out
loud? And not just get yourself labelled as something
you're not.

RICHARD: That's what I was saying.

BARBARA: As something you passionately loathe. And
find abhorrent. 'That's not me.' She said. 'That's not
me. But just by disagreeing... Maybe even by just
questioning—I will get myself lumped together with
all of *them.*'
(Then)
"So Barbara, how do I navigate through all of this," she
said, "and still stand up for myself, and still keep my
self-respect?"
(Then)

JANE: Who else was there in your backyard?

BARBARA: Just her. The two of us. My good friend
Margaret. One day last week after school.

TIM: Do I know Margaret?

BARBARA: You've seen her around, Tim. She teaches
science. I think, I hope, she felt a little better after
talking…

(Short pause)

RICHARD: Yvonne told us a story today.

BARBARA: Which story? She tells so many. They're all
so interesting.

RICHARD: *(To BARBARA)* Her friend's show that got shut
down…

BARBARA: Oh tell them that. Tell them… Listen to this. I
was just thinking of this too, Richard.
(Stands)
I'm going to get some water…

RICHARD: I'll wait…

BARBARA: *(Going)* You don't have to. Tell them… You
need anything?

RICHARD: I'm fine. Thanks.

(BARBARA goes off.)

RICHARD: It's about a friend of Yvonne's who was in a
show, in Canada.

JANE: Yvonne's Canadian, Tim.

TIM: I didn't know that.

RICHARD: And this play, it was about the struggles
and repression of indigenous Canadians. And the
nightmare they've lived, are living. To shed light on
that…. All good intentions… It was an interracial
company of actors, and they'd done plays set all over
the world. Different cultures. So they were taken aback

when they were accused of racism, because there were no indigenous actors hired to be in this play.

(BARBARA *has returned with her water.*)

RICHARD: But there were no indigenous actors in their interracial company. So there was a big blow up and, the show was cancelled; the government pulled its money… *(To* BARBARA*)* Yvonne seemed to really want to talk about this.

BARBARA: She did, Richard.

RICHARD: Like your friend Margaret.

BARBARA: Yeh.

RICHARD: *(Continues)* The theater company, they all tried to defend themselves. But of course their defense— 'that we are all one people' — 'a common humanity' —that's completely suspect right now. The head of the theater company even wrote a letter to the newspaper and said something like 'cultures are not the property of anyone. They seed each other. And always have.' 'We all have eyes, ears, memories, legends. We are not just this, and not just that.'

JANE: Good luck.

TIM: So what happened?

BARBARA: The show was cancelled.

TIM: I mean, did anyone respond to that letter? You write that here, now, and people would respond…

JANE: Oh that's true.

RICHARD: They did, Tim. They really did. In droves, Yvonne said. And it all got very ugly… The theater director's letter, of course, just got drowned out. Lost in the angry noise…

TIM: Right.

RICHARD: And so that's how it ended.

(Then)

Yvonne said her friend called her up late one night, woke Yvonne up. Her friend said she couldn't sleep. She was trying to understand her feelings about all of what happened.

(Then)

She said, 'being accused of racism is a very scary thing. I find myself just shutting down.'

(Then)

BARBARA: That's like what Margaret was saying.

(To RICHARD*)*

And that's what made me think of Yvonne's story.

(Then)

So—is that the goal of some people now, who accuse you—to shut you down? To get you so scared, that you just shut yourself down?

RICHARD: Not everyone.

I said, some people.

(Short pause)

TIM: I sit here in my house—my Mom's house. In this room where I—. I studied for the S A Ts in this chair where I'm sitting. I remember digging into this desk with the point of a compass. I learned lines for the first play I was ever in—in school. Right here. Francis Nurse in *The Crucible*…

JANE: *(To the others)* That's an old man. I'd pay anything to have seen Tim as—

TIM: I was terrible, Jane. I told you.

JANE: *(Over the end of this)* Why do you think I want to see it?

TIM: *(Continues)* My books are still on the shelf. From school. From college… While I've been here, I've been

taking them down, looking through them, reading what I'd underlined as a kid…
(Then)
And I've been thinking… That's what I've told myself I ought to do.

JANE: Thinking about what?

TIM: I'll show you…
(He grabs a book.)
Here…I've gone through this. Everything I underlined as a nineteen-year-old…

RICHARD: What is it? The book?

TIM: Baldwin. James Baldwin…
(It is Notes Of A Native Son.)
(As he thumbs through) So much of what he says, it's what you're hearing, from young people especially, people of color… Right now. He said fifty years ago or more. To look back into history, at the crimes. Here… My younger self underlined this… *(Reads)* "The conundrum of color is the inheritance of every American, be he/she legally Black or White. It is a fearful inheritance."
(Turns pages)
Here, I underlined a lot in his introduction. I probably was writing a paper… He wrote this intro years after the book, when it was being reissued… So Baldwin's sixty now. And he's looking back. Here, he lists things he loves and dislikes…I have three check marks beside this. So this made an impression on young me.
(Paraphrases)
Baldwin loves to eat. Loves to
(Reads)
"argue with people who do not disagree with me too profoundly."

RICHARD: Me too!

JANE: The same…

TIM: *(Paraphrases from the book)* He loves—to laugh, Barbara…

BARBARA: And Jane…

TIM: *(Paraphrases)* He doesn't like
(Reads)
"people who are earnest". He doesn't like people who like him
(Reads)
"because I'm a Negro, nor do I like people who find me contemptible for that same 'accident.'" His word. The nineteen-year-old underlined that twice. Then he says, and I have to quote this: "I love America more than any other country in the world, and exactly for this reason, I insist on the right to criticize her perpetually."
(Then)
I hadn't underlined that. I just came across that last night…
(Then)
(Paraphrases)
He says that for him all theories are suspect.
(Reads)
"Because even the finest principles may be pulverized"
—his word— "by the demands of life." And so, therefore, quoting again,
(Reads)
"one must find one's own moral center and move through the world hoping that this center will guide one aright."

RICHARD: So the older, now sixty-year-old man, is saying in an introduction to his young self: that life is complicated…

BARBARA: Uh-huh.

RICHARD: I like that.

TIM: I do think that's what he's saying. And I think that's what my nineteen-year-old self wasn't interested in and so it wasn't underlined. But I am interested in that now… It's good to hear that now… From him.
(Then)
Others I'm sure read this and hear other things. Very different things. That's often the case with a great writer…

BARBARA: That's why we need great writers.

TIM: We do. One more, okay?
(He grabs a notebook.)

JANE: You've been spending a lot of time in your old room, Tim.

TIM: I have, Jane… The girls ignore me. My mom's in a home. You can't go anywhere…
(Finds what he is looking for in a notebook.)
Here. I told you I've been looking through my old books. And copying stuff into here. This book I don't think I even read.

BARBARA: Who?

TIM: A playwright. His name is Athol Fugard, Barbara.

RICHARD: I don't know him.

JANE: Yvonne might.

RICHARD: She might.

TIM: I think she would. I've been reading it the last couple of days. Here. Let me read this that the old me has copied out.
(Reads)
"This country is in the grip of its worst drought—and that is in the human heart. So my country needs to be loved now, when it is at its ugliest, more than at any other time."
(Closes the notebook)

He's South African. He wrote this in the midst, the 'heyday', of apartheid… He's white. Athol Fugard.
(Then)
I was so moved when I came across this quote yesterday that I sent it off to a friend without thinking. And that is what he wrote back.

RICHARD: What?

TIM: 'Fugard's white.'
(Then)
And that's why that story your girlfriend told, Richard… Right away, when you were telling it, I wondered if those actors were maybe just a bit naïve?

RICHARD: What do you mean?

TIM: That kind of thinking— 'we're all one'. My friend would certainly say, those times have changed. He'd say, 'They're white.' 'White saviors trying to turn themselves into 'white victims.'

RICHARD: Is that fair?

TIM: That is what I think he would say. My friend. Fair or not. Be careful where you tell that story…

(Short pause)

BARBARA: You know, as I grew older I thought the world would get bigger, not smaller…I believed that.

JANE: What do you mean smaller?

BARBARA: You know I've talked about travel. Visiting places. Egypt say. Greece. Vietnam. My horizons to be widened. The possibilities that are out there. And I would feel a part of all that. Part of some great big goddamn humanity…

TIM: Good luck.

BARBARA: I know. Instead it feels to me like we're making it all smaller and smaller. Cutting up this,

dividing it into that. This is—yours, this is mine. These
are the lines. These are the borders. The walls. Don't
cross them. Or cross them at your own risk...
(Then)
Doesn't that just reduce who we are? And so *we*
become smaller and smaller...

RICHARD: I dreamed that I was shrinking. I'm in a
chair, drinking coffee, and suddenly the coffee mug
gets bigger and bigger, and the chair too, the window,
because, in my eyes, I'm getting smaller... So I start to
blow hard and harder...
(He demonstrates.)
Like I'm pumping up a balloon, but that balloon is
me... And pretty soon I'm back to normal size.
(Smiles)

BARBARA: *(A joke, to* JANE*)* I wonder what that's about?
Jane, his eye problem has come back.

JANE: Richard—

RICHARD: Past month.

BARBARA: He didn't want to say anything.

RICHARD: I now have a large 'nowhere' in my left eye,
bottom right corner. So objects suddenly disappear,
and then come back, come out of the blue...I'm trying
to get used to that. That that's the new normal.

JANE: Tim, you know the dream I mentioned? The
first one I've had that I remember having, since I got
depressed. Since my depression.

TIM: You know you've never said that word... Not to
me...

JANE: 'Depression.' And I'm not alone. There's a
pandemic.

TIM: I know that.

JANE: I dreamed that I'd been ordered by someone to take away all the color in our apartment here. Everything that had color had to go… So we'd be left in black in white. The books, the rugs…the couch I covered in a white sheet…I was told, only on my birthday, could I have any color back…
But my birthday was still months away… So I'd have to wait…

(Then)

I remember saying to you, Tim, in the dream: I'll manage. I can wait. Just as long as I know there's something to wait for.

(Then)

TIM: At the bar where I'm now working.

RICHARD: You're working? In Amherst?

JANE: He took a job, Richard.

RICHARD: What are you talking about?

TIM: I'm doing a favor for a friend from high school. He owns this bar. It's not a job.

RICHARD: You have a job in Rhinebeck.

TIM: Someone's filling in for me.

RICHARD: *(Over this)* Aren't you coming back?

JANE: I don't know that, Richard.

TIM: I said I was, Jane…

JANE: When?

TIM: I'm coming back, come on.

BARBARA: Tim, Marian was just talking to us, before her date. I'm going to tell him, Jane. Marian offered to take in both Karen and Maggie. She has room. She has Evan's old room. And a yard. *(A joke)* She has games, she said. Didn't she?

JANE: She said that.

BARBARA: And she means it. She said she could teach them both how to drive. She never got to do that with Evan…

TIM: That's very generous. It's a thought. I can't stay here…

JANE: That's good to know.

TIM: And I want to come home.

JANE: That's good to know.

TIM: Barbara, I'll ask the girls…

JANE: When?

BARBARA: Make it sound like fun.

TIM: I will. But it's up to the girls…

JANE: Of course.

TIM: Anyway, Richard, I was saying, at my job here, which isn't a job, more like a favor to an old friend—

JANE: He's being paid.

TIM: *(Over this)* I ran into my high school drama teacher. He's still teaching…

BARBARA: Hard to get rid of us old ones.

RICHARD: The pandemic's trying…

TIM: He gave me a copy of—and you're going to think I'm crazy, because I know I've talked a lot about it already. You're going to think I'm obsessed. *The Cherry Orchard*.

RICHARD: Oh my god. Tim.

JANE: What more is there to say?

BARBARA: Let him talk, Jane.

TIM: He told me that there was a scene cut in its first production. And it's a beautiful scene. He didn't know why it was cut. In it the old servant tells a story about when he was a young boy on a wagon with his dad, and they're taking a bunch of sacks of something— wheat, oats, I don't know—in the wagon. And the servant as a boy looks back at the sacks, at all these dead things…

JANE: And what?

TIM: When in one of them, one of the sacks, something inside, wiggles. Just wiggles. That's what he remembers. Just remembers it going 'Wiggle-wiggle.' Was there rat? A bug? Who knows?
(Then)
Just when you think there's nothing… There's still something. You think it's all gone, and then something suddenly—. Something's still alive…

(Lights fade.)

4.
Art.

(BARBARA, RICHARD, JANE and TIM.)

(As LUCY MICHAEL appears on her screen.)

LUCY: Barbara, I'm so sorry! I fell asleep.

BARBARA: *(Over this)* Lucy!

LUCY: Am I too late?

BARBARA: We're still here. We're here.

LUCY: *(Over this)* Fuck. I am so sorry. I apologize. This never ever happens to me. I'm never late!

BARBARA: *(Over the end of this)* I know. I know you, Lucy. It's okay. It's okay.
(Introducing)
Richard. Lucy Michael.

RICHARD: Hi. Nice to meet you.

BARBARA: Tim… Jane's boyfriend.

JANE: *('A joke')* Is that who he is?

BARBARA: You know Jane. You need to warm up? If you do—.

LUCY: I was warmed up, Barbara, then I feel asleep.

BARBARA: You're not that late. Take your time. Take your time. We've got nothing else to do. *(To the others)* The prize I won. My gift to all of you!

(They all watch her warm up for a moment:)

LUCY: How's Rhinebeck, Barbara? I miss it.

BARBARA: I'm in Albany. Helping my brother pack. He's moving to Rhinebeck. What time is it in France now?

LUCY: Three in the morning, Barbara.

RICHARD: Why is she in France?

BARBARA: Jesus Christ, no wonder you fell asleep. Who wouldn't fall asleep? How's the residency going?

JANE: Richard, she's doing a residency.

LUCY: We're back into the studios. That's good. That's progress. With masks…
(Warms up, then:)
Again, thank you for this. This summer's been a nightmare for my dancers in New York.

BARBARA: I can only imagine.

LUCY: Everyone's broke. Our auction helped a little…

BARBARA: Good.
(Then)
What dance did you choose?

LUCY: The one you asked for, Barbara, what did you think?

BARBARA: Your mother's. The one she taught you, you said.

LUCY: She did…

JANE: Tim, I saw this dance with Barbara in Catskill.

LUCY: There…I'm ready…

BARBARA: Do you talk a lot to your Mom? From France?

LUCY: We Skype. Not as often as I'd like… She sleeps a lot now. Have you gotten to see my Mom, Barbara?

BARBARA: She stays inside, Lucy. She has to…

LUCY: Of course. Obviously.

BARBARA: I'm sure all that's hard on you…

LUCY: It is… It is. And when it gets too much, you know what I do?

BARBARA: I can guess… You dance.

LUCY: You got it. So you ready? Then I guess I'll just dance. Could you all mute yourselves? The music gets a little crazy otherwise….
All set? Then here we go…

(She turns on the music from her i-phone.)

(Music: Scott Joplin's Maple Leaf Rag.*)*

(And LUCY *begins to dance, in a cramped space, Dan Wagoner's* Brokenhearted Rag.*)*

(Approximately 3 minutes of dance.)

*(*LUCY *finishes, the others still muted, applaud unheard. She gestures that they muted. They unmute and:)*

OTHERS: Take a bow! Lucy, take a bow! Take a bow!! A bow!

*(*LUCY *takes a slight bow.)*

BARBARA: *(Very excited)* She was my student! I'm so proud.

RICHARD: You taught her to dance?

BARBARA: Shut up. I taught her English.

OTHERS: A bigger bow! Come on! A big bow! A real one!
Don't be shy...

(As LUCY *takes a big bow, and they applaud:)*

(Lights fade.)

5.
The Right to Whisper.

*(*RICHARD, BARBARA, TIM *and* JANE. LUCY *is saying goodbye, waving.)*

OTHERS: Thank you. Thank you, Lucy!

BARBARA: Lucy, it was beautiful!

LUCY: Goodnight. Thank you.

OTHERS: Goodnight!!

BARBARA: Go to bed!

*(*LUCY *signs off.)*

(Then)

TIM: I needed that. I needed a little art in my day. Thank you, Barbara.

BARBARA: I think we all did.

JANE: Tim, when do you have to go to your 'job'?

TIM: It's not a job. *(Change of subject)* The kids—

JANE: They're not kids.

TIM: Karen and Maggie. They should see some art. I could take them to MASS MOCA one of these days. It's open now.

RICHARD: You need reservations…

TIM: Then I'll make them, Richard. That was my Mom's and my place to go together. She loved taking me there. Be nice to see some art in person.

JANE: It would.

BARBARA: I agree.

RICHARD: Yvonne has said the same thing…

TIM: Jane, I found a journal my mother's been keeping. Was keeping, until she went into the home. It'd been left in my room. I think she was sleeping sometimes in here. So in this little book, she names the day of the week, so say Monday, and she lists what she does. Teeth brushing. Takes three pills. Washes a pair of underwear that got stained. Reads five pages of *War and Peace*. At the very end she'd gotten as far as page 212. Everything that she eats. Cooks. T V shows watched. Who calls. Nothing about feeling worried or scared. Just the stuff she does.
(Then)
It made me sad. I figured she must have started it when she first felt she was getting forgetful. She wasn't a sad person at all. Isn't… This morning, I'm in bed and I open it again, read little more, and folded up in one of the back pages is a flier from an art show. London, Tate Modern. "The Paintings of Pierre Bonnard." With this subtitle, which she'd circled: "Incidental Moments of the Day". That's what he painted.
(Then)

Maybe it isn't sad. Maybe what she was doing was—like Bonnard—recording, and maybe finding meaning, maybe beauty in all the little things of her day...

JANE: Can you ask her, Tim?

TIM: Not anymore.

(BARBARA *gets up.*)

BARBARA: I want more wine...

RICHARD: I can get...

(BARBARA *goes.*)

JANE: Richard, Tim's going to have to go.

RICHARD: Jane, you think Marian is serious about taking the girls?

JANE: I think so.

RICHARD: Is that a good idea, Tim?

TIM: I'll have to ask.

JANE: They'd have their own room. Not like having to share with me. With my office. She has a house. A yard.

TIM: I know the selling points. I'll do my best. I'll ask. (*Then*)
Richard, before Barbara comes back, how is she doing?

RICHARD: What do you mean?

TIM: With Yvonne. I can't tell. She's Barbara.

RICHARD: She... She hardly says anything.

JANE: Barbara?

RICHARD: Yeh. When she's around Yvonne. She's very quiet. Yvonne keeps telling stories just to keep the conversation going. I try too. She keeps trying to pull Barbara out of her shell. That's what she calls it. I tell her, once Barbara gets to know you...

JANE: I think Barbara's worried about being alone.

RICHARD: She's been alone for a long time. I've only been in her house since March.

JANE: And Yvonne will come to Rhinebeck with you?

RICHARD: Maybe.

JANE: You and Barbara have been like an old couple, Richard.

RICHARD: Yvonne told me a story just now in the car…

JANE: Another Yvonne story.

RICHARD: A theater company in Germany, she has a friend in it. There is not one female actor over the age of thirty-seven. There were men in their fifties, sixties, one in his seventies. Yvonne said 'Richard, you men have no idea the life we live…' She said in the context of talking about—.

(BARBARA *returns with her wine and a beer.*)

BARBARA: In case you needed another beer. I opened a new bottle. Hopefully one of your very very special ones. It had a cork.

TIM: I do need to go.
(*He starts to stand, stops.*)
Jane… What Karen said to you, she knows that was wrong.

JANE: She said that?

TIM: Yes.

JANE: I'm not sure I believe you.

TIM: It was a very unfair and nasty thing to say.

JANE: I agree.

TIM: She'll apologize. Now, here, another look at my childhood bedroom. The things that happened here.

And, Jane, the things I said to my Mother here…
Unforgiveable. But—she forgave me. Love you. Night.

BARBARA: Goodnight.

TIM: Night. Thanks for the dance, Barbara. Nice
change… Great gift.

JANE: Love you.

TIM: Love you.
(He closes his computer. He is gone.)

BARBARA: I hope Marian is having a good time on her
date.

JANE: And he actually has a nose… Her date.

BARBARA: By now she's found out.

(RICHARD's phone rings.)

BARBARA: That's your phone, not mine.

RICHARD: I know. *(Looking at his phone, to BARBARA)*
It's— *(Into phone)* Hi…

BARBARA: *(Over this)* I know. I know who it is…

(RICHARD stands.)

BARBARA: *(Mouths to JANE)* 'Yvonne.'

RICHARD: *(Into phone)* It was beautiful. It's over. Good
timing. We videoed it.
(Answering a question)
For you. Who do you think?

BARBARA: Can you take that into the other room,
please?

RICHARD: *(Into phone)* I'm going into the other room…
Yvonne says hi.

JANE: Hi Yvonne…

BARBARA: Hi.

(RICHARD goes.)

BARBARA: Last week, this is funny, I copied what you and Tim do, and took a walk by myself in the cemetery. I came across this family plot. I forget the name. So there were all these little gravestones, this name on that and that name on this, dates, birth, death. Then at the corner of the plot there was one very small gravestone, only one word on it, no name, no dates, one word. This word: 'Aunt'.

(Then)

I want to at least have 'Teacher' on mine too.

(Then)

JANE: He really wants you to like her, Barbara.

BARBARA: Yvonne?

JANE: He said he wants his sisters to like her. He wants to 'bring her into the family.'

BARBARA: Then we'll drag her in...

JANE: But 'don't suffocate' her. He said that too. Have you gotten out of him how long he's known her for?

BARBARA: I figured as much as two years. I heard him say they met after he came back from an Adirondack vacation. He took that two years ago...

JANE: Two years. Wow. We are bad sisters. We need to snoop better.

BARBARA: And what did Karen say to you, Jane?

(No response)

BARBARA: You'll get over it.

(Then)

At lunch yesterday at Yvonne's... At her very nice house.

JANE: Is it really that nice?

BARBARA: *(Shrugs)* I don't know. And Yvonne got talking about Benjamin. Wait until you meet her,

you'll see, she just talks and talks and talks. Hardly lets anyone else have a chance. They'd been in two or three plays together. The first one she was just an understudy… But he'd been
(Voice:)
'so kind to me.'

JANE: Of course. Benjamin.

BARBARA: She told me the play and I'd actually seen it. I remember it. I tell Yvonne that, and she up and goes and pulls out a copy of the play with Benjamin's picture on the cover… And she insists on giving it to me… Let me get it…
(As she gets it:)
(Off)
She read me a speech from the play… She said she used to watch him from the wings every day give this speech…
(Returns with the book)
She said it was
(Voice)
'so Benjamin Apple.' Here, take a look:
(Shows the book cover)

JANE: *(Looking at the book cover)* Benjamin. Look at him, Barbara. Put it closer. He's so young…

BARBARA: I know. She read the speech well. Not showy, I expected showy or flowery like her dresses. What's amazing is I remember him, saying some of this, when he couldn't remember anything. It would just come out. Here, he'd say this:
(Reads)
"We only visit each other to bitch about how it's hard for us to live. But for God's sake, don't take that away, our last means of existing, allow us to say, 'it's hard for us to live.' Even like this, in a whisper:

(Whispers)
'it's hard for us to live.' I ask you on behalf of a million
people: "Give us the right to whisper."
(Looks up)
Jane, he'd say it right out of the blue. He'd be sitting,
staring off and then in a whisper, "Give us the right to
whisper…" Benjamin…

*(*MARIAN *appears on her screen.)*

MARIAN: I'm back!

JANE: Marian!

MARIAN: We didn't go to the Beekman. He took me to
Gaby's.

BARBARA: *(Over this)* How was the date? Does he have
a nose?

MARIAN: He has a nose, but the chin's not so great.

JANE: You were looking forward to the Beekman.

MARIAN: Gaby's—outside. So you basically eat in
a parking lot. It was different. Anything would be
different.

BARBARA: Marian, you missed the dance…

JANE: It was beautiful…

MARIAN: Good. I took his picture. He didn't notice, he
was paying the bill…Jane, what are you doing now?

JANE: I'm just home.

MARIAN: You want me to come on over? I can come
over.

JANE: I do want to hear—

BARBARA: Do it.

MARIAN: Let me get changed. And get out of this
dress…Barbara?
(She starts to go.)

BARBARA: I'm in Albany, Marian.

MARIAN: Right. I won't stay long.
(As she goes)
Where's Richard?

BARBARA: *(Calls)* On the phone with his girlfriend…

MARIAN: Jane, you sure it's okay? You're not busy?

JANE: Duh. What do I have to do? What are you talking about?

MARIAN: Bye, Barbara…
(She is gone.)

BARBARA: Wear a mask… She just had dinner with a stranger. Be careful.

JANE: I know. She wants to talk.

BARBARA: Must have gone well… She had fun. She's in a good mood. Take notes…

JANE: I will.

BARBARA: You better go get ready for Marian. And I need to clean up here, do the dishes. Those two can be on for hours.

JANE: And you'll be back tomorrow.

BARBARA: I will. Bright and early.

RICHARD: *(Off, calls)* Barbara, Yvonne's asked me over for a drink, do you mind?

BARBARA: *(Calls)* No. Of course not.
(She looks at her watch.)

RICHARD: *(Over the end of this)* You sure it's all right?
(He has gone.)

BARBARA: *(Calls)* Why are asking me? I'm not your mother.

RICHARD: *(From off)* I'll do the dishes when I'm back…!

(Short pause)

*(*JANE *and* BARBARA *look at each other.)*

(Then:)

JANE: You going to be all right?

BARBARA: *(Smiles)* Are you?
(Then)
I need to go to the bathroom…

(Then)

JANE: And Marian's coming over.

BARBARA: Right. Hug.

JANE: Hug… Love you. Thanks for the dance.

BARBARA: Love you.

JANE: 'Night.

BARBARA: 'Night.

*(*JANE *closes her computer.)*

*(*BARBARA *is alone, she looks at herself in the computer for a moment, drinks her water, then signs off.)*

END OF PLAY